The Martini Diet

The Martini Diet

Gaylord Brewer

Dream Horse Press
California

Library of Congress Cataloging-in-Publication Data:

Brewer, Gaylord
The Martini Diet

p. cm

ISBN 978-0-9777182-3-8
1. Poetry

10 9 8 7 6 5 4 3 2 1

First Edition

Cover: "Martini Shadow" photograph by Ryan McCormack,
http://www.docrpm.com

For J.,

1991 - 2006—

we were yours

Acknowledgments

Sections I and IV of this manuscript were written at the Obras Arts Centre in the rural Alentejano region of Portugal during the summer of 2005. Section II was written the previous summer, during a second residency at Hawthornden Castle in Scotland, and includes the final apologias from a 2+ year period during which I wrote nothing else. Thanks to my enduring hosts and caretakers. Section III was written in the fall of 2004, when I was teaching sophomore lit. for the first time in years. Except for the Hemingway stories (and possibly a Williams poem or two), which kicked the door open on their own, all the works tortured here for my conceits appear in *The Bedford Introduction to Literature*, 7th ed. Ironically, or perhaps just luckily, Michael Meyer published one of the pieces in the *Bedford*'s next edition. Section V includes the most recent poems, written back in Tennessee.

Thanks to the editors of the publications where the following poems appeared:

Agni: "The Hunter and the Figs"; *The Alembic*: "Blue-Eyed Boy," "Dinner Out"; *Alimentum*: "The Black Pigs"; *Briar Cliff Review*: "Apologia to the Blue Tit," "Men with Swimming Pools"; *Broken Bridge Review*: "Ashes"; *The Cape Rock*: "Her Tippet, Only Tulle"; *Carolina Quarterly*: "Miss Emily's Men"; *Chatauqua Literary Journal*: "Fold the Map Away"; *Cimarron Review*: "I Will Listen"; *Cincinnati Review*: "Apologia for 23 Postcards, Unwritten," "The Plums in the Icebox"; *Connecticut Review*: "Hemingway This Morning"; *Cooweescoowee*: "Burning," "Only Insomnia"; *Dos Passos Review*: "A Pretty Thing to Do"; *Emrys Journal*: "Apologia for Trying to Read Ted Hughes with Comfort in Mind"; *Epicenter*: "The CEO of Poetry"; *Florida Review*: "The Flaw," "Three Ghosts in Évora"; *Margie*: "The Woman"; *New Madrid*: "Burning," "Only Insomnia"; *Number One*: "Apologia for a Sunday Pre-empted by Foxes," "Apologia for the After-Breakfast Nap"; *Poem*: "Wolves, Bears, No Cops"; *Poetry Miscellany*: "Apologia for the Storm I Carry"; *Portland Review*: "For Sónia Matias, Portuguese Bullfighter"; *Prairie Schooner*: "Blackberries," "Duck Confit," "First Day out of the Box"; *Quarterly West*: "Apologia for Airport Farewells," "Apologia to the Green Man"; *River Styx*: "Apologia to the Blue Tit"; *Rockhurst Review*: "Colosseum by Moonlight," "Yes, the Amontillado"; *Santa Fe Literary Review*: "Ashes"; *Smartish Pace*: "Men, Building" (nominated for Pushcart Prize XXXII); *Southern Poetry Review*: "Apologia for Leaving"; *Xavier Review*: "Apologia for Missing My Wife's Call while Inspecting the Carcass of a Tawny Owl," "Repair."

"Apologia to the Blue Tit" was included in *Best American Poetry 2006* (Scribners).

"The Joys of Secret Sin" appeared in *The Bedford Introduction to Literature*, 8th edition, and "Night in the Body" in the Knoxville Writers' Guild anthology *Low Explosions: Writings on the Body*.

The author is grateful to the Faculty Development Committee and the Faculty Research and Creative Activity Committee, Middle Tennessee State University, for awards that assisted in the completion of this book.

I love to bleed. Sometimes I love to bleed so much, I take a beating.

—Arturo Gatti

Contents

IV: Men, Building

V: Home Fires

I: The Obras

until I sang with a savaged mouth,
like a corpse, in the grapes of the earth.

—*Pablo Neruda*

The Black Pigs

They live days rooting fenced fields,
quiet, predestined days of grunt or squeal,
stiff-gallop after the afternoon train
then fall again to idleness or reflection.
In early evening, before the kestrel
arrives to commence its solitary rituals,

I amble over rail tracks to join them,
expound my theories on the dead and briefly
living. They are patient, practical pigs
and pass me in ragged file, a few twisting
magnificent stubbled snouts to scent
my arguments through rungs of fencing.

Soon enough, it is back to burrowing
dust and scraggy creekbed for whatever
unlikely insight might avail itself
until last blessèd months of acorn
before the knife. Philosophy a pig can use.
For me, back for a hot scrub,

a secular sacrament. The cotton of bread
weighted with thin slices of my hosts,
striated, beautiful, darker than the wine,
trimmed neatly but not excessively
by the Saturday pork-monger who wishes
for me always a good week. The ribbon

of fat thick and white, brined flesh
an indulgent perfection. I lick fingers
clean of this wildly expensive grease
then ruin them for another bite,
teeth cutting easily the encasing crust,
rending meat delicately into strips.

I mouth the grape's blood, consider
my porcine brothers small in the distance.
When the hawk arrives from the west,
holding, fluttering, limned and hungry
against a fading bow of dusk, another day
is nearly lost forever, very nearly.

Upon My Hiking Two Hours Up Évoramonte to Find a Public Telephone, You Don't Answer

Instead, I listen to my own voice
and squirm at how
the brief recording seems extended,
how coins click away
in time to my strained intonation
to leave a message. I squint down
at new sandals, orange with dust,
down at the hamburger
of feet raw between
Italian leather ribs. The walk back,
though downhill, is no shorter.

Beyond the glass
of this capsule, this upright,
open-sided coffin spinning
through space, the men
dot the square, silent with their dark
caps and canes, staring at me
staring at them.
For all our benefit I turn a shoulder,
bow head for privacy.

At last the mealy voice shuts up.
I wait for the beep, then,
as the money runs out, tell myself
three times how I love me,
how I miss me and hope I'm well.

For Sónia Matias, Portuguese Bullfighter

Less coarsely, *cavaleiro*, despite
confused gender. I, too, was confused.
But as your steed tucked hind legs
and lifted in the first balletic spiral
you commanded, all was forgiven.
The horse's groomed plaits
merely echo of your own golden mane,
cascading from a single black ribbon
the length of your brocaded satin
coat. By the time you raised furry
tri-cornered hat to dedicate
the evening's work to us, this dusty,
loud-mouthed assembly in Azaruja,
I felt already the tempest of your gaze
parting locals to find me. Your first *farpa*
landed a bit low in the shoulder,
the second, I thought, a tad high.
What matter?! Brilliantly you held
the saddle of your Lusitanian, boots
glowing, agile, sure against flank,
bounce proud as you taunted sheathed horn
and blood rose in your cheek.

By the time, that is, a third flag unfurled,
its point penetrated squarely
into thick hump of animal muscle,
by then you were perfection.
It was a long evening, a hard one.
The blinding temperature fell
with the sun, and as you circled
the ring for final tribute, we learned again
the chill of each defeated day.
I did not toss my cap onto the sand then,
to be smoothed by your hand and returned,
nor red shirt, nor sandal, nor bouquet

of lily and tulip. We required no such
vulgarities. The tired splendor
of your smile contained, I knew,
a salt-sweet improbability of happiness,
that this was true *fado*, the fate
you passed to me. A song
in short that you could not love a poet.
Couldn't watch from the crowd the outcome
of each deadly *tourada* with language,
dangerous verbal bravura
ritualized each afternoon. The words,
you feared, would tame and destroy you.

I understood. I even—dark-eyed
dancer on hooves and deliverer
of the dart of spectacle and pain—
I even agreed. After every photograph
was flashed, autograph signed, child
and father kissed, without any last look
in my direction, you stripped
to a simple white shirt and folded
into your Audi convertible. Without
a look—for who were we to indulge,
who traffic in artifice and desolation?—
you nodded to your boy to drive you
away. The night had arrived,
brought the cold we'd known was coming.
I sat at the curb in open sleeves,
resisted hugging myself, and waited
like a man waits for a taxi.

I Will Listen

when you confess again
unforgiving nights. Don't worry
whether I've heard before
or care. Perhaps I have
or haven't, do or do not.
Speak as if any witness could assist.
The luscious fevers,
although the room cools
with breeze, hot river
of your face for hours
indistinguishable from tears.
Perhaps such language is excusable.
Who may argue how the day
was bartered, what hush
thistle grass might have
warned of, what remains
the shrill owl demanded?
Was it leather or down, that flap
of great wing, real or frame
to one lost dream or another?
I will not judge you
when hand again lurches
for the cord, body tumbles
terribly upright, when
translucent feet trace
again a small circle of light.
I will listen and, perhaps,
some night join you in your paces,
sooth dry lips with water,
cross myself in your name.
Perhaps you will turn,
with that fear forever unclear
to you, as the door rattles
in its lock despite
a sudden calm. You'll know then
I've arrived, and welcome me.

Night in the Body

> To be faithful in storm, patient of fools, tolerant of
> memories and the muttering prophets,
> It is needful to have night in one's body.
>
> —*Robinson Jeffers*

The feet to begin,
text of their soldiering defeat,
encrypted demands.
A document of wound
on one side, wound the other.

The skin's flaming parchment.
How the sun marks,
how passes, how destroys.
How the chest burns beneath its pulse.

Then the night.
The billows of the sheet.
The summons of curtain.
The sky's cold vocabulary of fire.

The eyes closed
as if to contain, and lips,
parched and mute,
poised to inhale
language the voice will never speak.

And a faltered breath,
risen in the frame.

The Flaw

> What isn't changed
> for the worse each time I look at it, what perfection
> would remain without my gaze? The better part
> of all there is prefers that I not be—
> . . . the flaw that shows the art.
>
> —*Gabriel Spera*

Unearth the signs required
and stamp them in dirt:
he dreams of wolves dancing
snow, beneath a moon, yes,
then the bloody human
hooves. His meager tools,
ironies and faithlessness,
these are accommodations.
With his devil's eyes and clawed
hand, is he any different?
Awe, humility, shame,
words whispered
to fan the blaze. The last wolf
quartered for sport, viscera
left to stiffen, then to rot.
He boils an iron skillet
above a stingy fire,
rice for his mother and father,
but the small weevils swim up
the heat, one, another,
then pairs, giddily ruining
soft grains, the last
in the sack. He dumps the mess
for ants and can't begin again.
He wakes, reluctantly,
to orange lava, molten clay.
What is fear but recognition
of place? Pause. Breath.
With a flourish, he draws aside
the long curtain of morning.

Three Ghosts in Évora

Back to Lisboa, back to buses and rails,
back at last to a Chapel of Jaundiced Bones.
5000 monks can't be wrong, although
grins lack much bite. Shadowed sockets
see exactly as before, brittle crochets
of tibia still jitterbug in place.
These the cozy remembrances.
By pure fluke I am on the kid's scent again
this summer, trailing him even further.
I flash on the spot when I see it:
there he sits behind temple ruin,
posing on marble on the Largo Cutileiro,
turned and squinting over the city
as if contemplating a purchase. I know—
he thinks he can almost smell his life
blooming in those hills and beyond,
onto the sea and across. A sure thing.
Look at the waist, biceps bulged
in his flowered shirt, thin beard
and practiced gaze, gray pouch fresh
from the hockshop, fat with pens
and paper and lousy fiction. The whole day
a photograph and, baby, he's the subject.

How to knock sense into a head barely
twenty-one? You can't. He peers through me
like I'm not there. This punk will
never see the fist coming, I swear to you
on a stack of 5000 broken skulls. I stand,
dust my trousers, adjust beloved
WWII Austrian artillery bag on my shoulder—
a lot like the boy's, actually, but
a generation older. I'm staying in a swank
pensão for the month, not overnight
in an 8-euro flophouse cuarto for students,

and it's time to maneuver poolside
with glass of estate vinho to take notes
on what I've seen, and I've seen it all.

But as I beep the locks on the rental,
a stranger I hadn't noticed lurches
from the entrance of the Convento dos Lóios—
frou-frou pousada for doddering Americans—
to block my way. Wrinkled crow
in dark glasses—pushing sixty if a day—
with paunch, white beard, signature red nose
of a boozer. Trust me I know the type,
Fate's Lonely Traveler, but this fellow's
been ridden hard kilometers and put up wet.
As he fumbles the flap of a threadbare gray
purse—Lord knows what he's hustling—
and raises a right hand in my face,
I move around him like forsaken wind.
Out of my way, grandpa! I don't offer
handouts or directions, and as for advice,
here's some: take a long last look and forget.
You have your own problems. I'm gone.

Skin

I remove a petal of skin
from my leg with a thumbnail
and commend it to air.
Then another, tender parchment
torn from the landscape
of black hairs, drifted
to terrace tiles where,
I notice, quite a lot of me
accumulates. Both limbs
in question seem attractive—

masculine legs, tanned,
with forceful musculature,
even ragged edges of peel
lending to weathered, credible
appearance. Within and without
dead edges, texture and hue
of epidermal map appear the same,
and as I ponder the usefulness
of this discovery, or not,
I also listen politely

to my host discuss his wells,
his water's purities,
how deep they had to go.
An umbrella of heavy cotton
shields our faces from blistering
afternoon sun. 190 meters.
I nod and concentrate,
but over his shoulder I cannot
help hungry looks at the bikinied
17-year-old on her knees,

then on her belly, carefully
positioning a husk of snake
exhumed from the garden
and now apparently commanding

her absolute attention.
I wonder, however, if this startling
performance isn't for my benefit,
or general dispensation
to the universe, downy legs
and lip ring aside.

My friend shakes his head,
theorizes the country's drying up.
The girl rolls on her hip
to photograph the snake
at an upward angle, her ass
a supple bud displayed for all.
I detach a long shred
of myself—abandoned self, that is—
and ask the wind deliver me
for her discretion, or not.

Men with Swimming Pools

are troubled men, straw hats bowed
to the unreflecting murkiness
of dream. Eyes distant, resigned smiles
accept the fateful pit dug and paid for.
Holiday devotions are thermometer
and brush, net and hose, chlorine strip,
bowing in and out the chapel of the motor.

Tomorrow, they tell their guests,
tomorrow it will clear, for sure.
Of course they never swim themselves,
these men, publicly, but pace sidelines
with antiseptic mission, circle borders
of the algaed battlefield, lost.

One failed alchemist, money turned
to muck, distributes one more cup
of powder across the surface of the soup
and gently stirs a ten-foot spoon.
Tomorrow, he says, but tomorrow brings
only cloud, tiny tide scoffing
across the dead sea of his pride.

Today, meanwhile, a guest marks her page,
balances the edge to test water with a toe.
Brrr, it's cold, she says, then cools
red-rare limbs in a splashy drop
to the bottom. Her host crosses his arms
and, common of the damned, looks away,
perhaps toward a shimmering heaven
of eighteen emerald holes only he can see.

The CEO of Poetry

When I bound from the helipad,
ordering quiet, I'm relaxed already.
My birdie is 18 punishing holes
for a normal man, sunset mudsoak
richer than his thin new skin.
My one whiff of quaint local vintage
quaffs a case, my glass empties
the cellar. My nibble of foie gras
is the whole damned goose.

Don't lose weight over your place
in the concern, limited options,
if I know your name. Ten minutes
beneath the decrepit olive tree
—older than Wall Street—
on the hill, totaling the night,
and I own it all like a monk
mumbling in his monastery. As long
as I call the shot—I've blueprinted

for forever—the Door, to you,
remains closed. Knock and wail
all you like, what I conjure there
requires a sound-proofed chamber.
That's why a little R&R is crucial
in its place. Listen: we're talking
balance, lines of perspective,
exploiting one's natural gifts.
What you want and how you get it.

That's why my 16 hours in paradise
are worth a month to you.
My week, more than your lifetime.

42/8

The first figure represents days
from home, the second until my return.
Each night in place of prayer
I ponder the subtly shifted
axis of the next morning's divisions,
then, waking again, chisel
one stone from the wall I built myself,
tumble it over the mounting debris behind.

Soon, sure, I will reunite
with wife and dog, desk and garden,
familiar sunsets, arguments, quiet meals
of reconciliation. Soon, perhaps as you
read this, these tallies
will represent nothing more
than an abstract amusement, a dusty
record of longing. But not today.

Fold the Map Away

There will be no
dizzying ascent
of mountain passage,
no affair
with flirtatious sea,

no ferries to islands
and no secret cove
to free yourself
of all but tender skin.
Forget them,

convents
and private rooms,
fish charred and hot
on briny lips,
a table in the harbor,

seamed fisherman
unraveling encrusted net.
None of it happens,
not for you.
Fold map compact again

along worn edges
of your dreaming,
then pack your rags
and discard the rest—
coordinate and distance,

guiding text
on which accommodation
might suit you,
what you might afford
and how to ask.

Where you're going
no such advice
is required, or,
finally now the truth,
of any use at all.

II: Hawthornden, Redux

To the bone, the careless white bone, the excellence.

—*Robinson Jeffers*

Apologia for Airport Farewells

We had sworn we'd never suffer
another, so knowing what swears were for
discovered ourselves again
at the terminal, again marking life
by partings. The avoided moment
gained distinction, force, momentum,
then always arrived the same:
you to rise into the sky
to a partial home and a dog's
sloppy greeting, to tend the garden,
to report. For my part, remaining on
as note taker of the exotic,
pursuer of ever-vaguer serendipities.
We'd gotten better. Circular talk,
more assurances, failed bit of silliness.
The hug was certain, and your eyes,
though edged in red, behaved themselves.
I choked it down, choked it down,
stared for an eternal moment
at guards, attendants, x-rays,
the empty passage, and, as often before,
tried to imagine you on the other side
beginning on your way.
Then eternity passed, and I too,
forever ending and beginning
—anyway once more before never again—
with time to burn, time to slaughter,
time to maim and carry, I looked away
toward some gray, early road,
and turned.

Apologia for an Evening at the Bed & Breakfast, after Delivering My Wife to the Airport

> "To enjoy the benefits of this Bath Oil, pour under warm water, lie back, close your eyes and relax."

I closed my eyes. Closed them to the tall
canary-yellow walls with scalloped trim, wrought-
iron ceiling fixture with sculpted lily sockets,
pedestal sink. I lay back in the claw-footed tub,
back until my ears submerged in geranium-
oiled roiling warmth, the lavender-and-lemongrass-
shower-gel-with-vitamin-E-beads infused broth,
relaxed to the luxury-bluebell-bath-essence
(*fleur de bluebell bain moussant*, "Naturally Scottish")
song, the forgiving ripple of two melted scoops
of bath soak crystals with organic essential oils
(*huiles essentielles*) of orange and, again, geranium
(excessive?). After an indefinite time, I rose like
an old, rehydrated lion from his perfumed pond,
an apothecary of Arran Aromatics dripping
from beard and loin. I toweled in thick
cotton, then left that room for another. As I crossed
muted carpet I was startled, I admit, to glean in
the standing mirror, out of context of comfort and place,
the pale legs of my father, tapering to his peculiar,
bulging knees. Still, I kept on to the parted
window, selected a tangerine from the pewter bowl
so to complement the late-setting sun blushing
the bay. I inspected again the delicate genitalia
of the orchid on the sill, ingested dazing scent.
And as I bent discovered, in admiration of its maker's
adaptability, precision and expedient purpose, a web
newly laced at the frame's opening. Then I lay again,
eyes open, on the soft and silent bed.

Apologia to the Hawk at Rosslyn Chapel

The sky that Friday afternoon clear,
brushed fair enough to distinguish
ring of worn hills containing us,
thick blind of valley. A palpable wind
assailed the cliff's roughness.
At the chapel—their crumbled enigma
of Mason and saint, Christian, pagan,
righteous Templar—wedding party
assembled in open circle. A bagpiper's
invitation trembled in the blow,
but not like you: holding, holding place
above the cemetery, dipping from view
behind cracked wall of bracken,
blackberry, wild rose, then risen again,
suspended in still flight on a buffeting
ferocity matched to your own.
It was you I moved toward, hawk:
your compact beauty, your ceremony
of sacrificial mice, and the threnody
of your rapturous, hungry evensong.

Apologia to the Green Man

You've known it all already, with your squinty
mirth: I admire and more your mischievous
foliation, twiggy speech twisting from teeth,
pagan amusement offered as irony to a world
dumb and deaf under its ministry of saws.
I have removed you from your nail, so that I—
as strikes me fitting on this windy holy day,
as June branches toss on the leafy sea—
may caress your trails of viney, vatic wisdom,
your dimpled chin of stone, sometimes
my own forest of chest and naked belly.
They've asked a hundred times that I deliver you,
return you to your box for their amusement
over Sunday eggs. Instead, I stand at the fire,
press a finger to the warm char of wood.
In private circle of mirror, I fashion my face
as your primitive reflection: trellises of hawthorn
from nostrils, two more below black beard,
trinity of curls flowering forehead.
Soot oily from mortal flesh grains my thumb
with paths I've worn since birth. I'll hold you
to your word verdant knight, clever cat, just
as dared. Today your humor is anguish enough.

Apologia for 23 Postcards, Unwritten

Already tidily licked with a perforated face
of Elizabeth and her price, the *par avion*
decorations of the Royal Mail. It's not idleness,
entirely, that delays me—I regard the unsmudged
possibilities as I riffle this stiff deck.
Even to address the cards risks reducing
that apparently luminous evening of September 14,
1842, diminishing even further a teensy
Prince Albert in top hat, ascot, and cane,
left hand presenting the untrammeled valley
wild beyond the castle court, but the right,
and ah, the gaze, dedicated solely to the discretion
of his queen. How fine Victoria looks tonight
in her bonnet and pink dress, how young! I thumb
the stack, but the detailed, doll-like figures,
smaller than spring peas, remain immobile,
undisturbed, happily caught forever in the locket
of Sir William Allen's amber strokes.
I can only hope, when the cards are at last
dealt, their redundant wit posted and delivered,
that you, my distant associates and many admirers,
may just perceive, with no improper wisp
of jealousy curling above your hum-drum lives,
my little face, my tiny raised glove
from among the shadows of the royal attendants
(23 in all, by the way, one for you each)—
straight-faced and sated, aloof but deferential
in my shiny red coat, and accept this small tribute.
There I am, thinking of you as I try not to smile.

Apologia to the Blue Tit

> We rise, drop our faces
> in cold water, and face the prospects
> of a day like the last one from which we
> have not recovered.
>
> —*Philip Levine*

Your preposterous death I contained
entirely in my palm, gave meaning
that meant nothing. Your name no longer
tolerated humor. My hand trembled,
the arm, the body itself from the folds
of its nightly deviations. Soft lemon
of breast no wider than a fingertip.
Each dead wing I lifted and let drop.
Uncurled small talons, let grip air again.
You were still warm with a memory
of life, it occurred to me, and I held
your head—your azure cap, the dark line
of broken nape—carefully in a crucible
of bone and flesh, tendon, blood.
When a car turned down the long drive,
stuttering, gray, operated by a stranger,
why did I lower you in embarrassment,
study a sky promising plenty more trouble.
Why nod a greeting I didn't believe,
caught red-handed in my inspection
of beauty discarded and already rotting.
I laid you in a shaded knot of pine,
spears of cut grass as your pyre,
resumed the timely errands of the day.

Apologia for the After-Breakfast Nap

Organs warmed by porridge, jam,
and tea, one may return attention
to the matter of the body's drowsy shell,
chilly spirit. One may, pushed away
from table, having offered oblique
farewells and forecasts, leave the reader
to his news, the walker to paths,
the scribbler to her pens and pads.
Returned to the garret, one may then
resuscitate the fire, silence accusing
ticks of any tiny alarm, let morning
clothes drop loose again to floor
and at last mount one's ship of blankets,
pillow-embrace, and scattered dream.
Floating atop a rumbling current
of logs, peering between reflections
at undulating horns of flame gilding
shadows in gold, one may ponder
this as a grateful act, an act of love.
Now, mind you, this person would not be me,
hunched over the business of society,
initiating a week's embroiled industry—no.
But for all I know, friend, it could be you,
surrendering the field and knowing
perfectly well what's good for you
in your soft, shameless, acquiescent glow.

Apologia for a Sunday Pre-empted by Foxes

For weeks I have traipsed
these wet strips of forest—
a skeleton at the river,
crushed eggshell, droppings,
scurried shadows. The moment
arrives, always, as a shock:
approaching my window
above the broken courtyard,
hoping for a clearer day,
hoping honestly for nothing much.
Then: *Gesture. Color. Shape.*
Brain flashing and discarding,
the gasp, sudden focus,
body charged and I recognize
it all in crystallized time:
first figure, rabbit limp in mouth,
second trotting pursuit
as if a couple in June dance
tracing cut circles of lawn.
I think *how red, how brilliant.*
Then they're gone, jaunty
leap after another into bramble
and faded rhododendron,
into ridge of sycamore,
beech, poplar that's still theirs.
Clouds—at that moment I swear—
part into grubby gray arms,
pulsing sun ignites each leaf
with a precise, glistening
intelligence and I'm running
the hallway, I'm breathing hard
with the urgency of witness.

Apologia for Trying to Read Ted Hughes with Comfort in Mind

> The poems, like smoking entrails,
> Came soft into your hands.

Strident verse of fire
warming one side,
heater in reach
at the other. Thick socks,
hot plate of soup.
Breaches to shameful
ease: the prickle
of exposed calf and knee,
window open to rain.
I frown again at the photo
of the living husband
—hair wild, eyes
dark, tweed and tie.
Then I poke the logs a bit,
logs I split
and trimmed to size
in last night's
failed light, with ax
of sufficient heft and edge
to require damage.
Smoke lingers in the soft
cavity of my shirt,
oily hands of flesh.
I prod and poke
and play my angles
to ensure the sizzle stays
the flame.

Apologia for the Storm I Carry

In the coffin of waters, hands crossed,
I heard an urgent heart, ragged breath
of an animal I knew. I kept good company
until the bath boiled and stank of the dying.
On the trail, I brought wind with me
in pocket and trousers, chest and hands
as ash and elder writhed, parted, bent low
to where I passed. What lay behind
lay in ruin, and all ahead trembled
at the feathered tempest hungry on my shoulder.
Even then I prayed to know, to be a better man,
appealed to the only god I'd ever believed.
When was it different? Did I acknowledge
my cry, did I give a damn, did I even exist
to reply in the dark thunder of my laughter?

Apologia for Missing My Wife's Call while Inspecting the Carcass of a Tawny Owl

Something had been at it again.
Buzzard, fox, or unknown.
Its identity a guess—when I lifted
detached head to roadside
in the afternoon, eyes, untufted ears
all missing, skull chewed clean
to wig of loose, matted skin.
In pale light the head gone,
breastbone raw. Only black, inch-long
talons, curled, sharp and limp,
reminded of what had been, irony
of hunter hunted. I hadn't intended
to miss your call, I can't believe that,
nor explain why I chose that moment
to step without speaking from
the table and others. On my last night
here a decade ago, I'd gone
breathless as a massive silhouette
spread silently at my approach
and rose into dark wood.
Now another last, guts and massacre.
I tell myself it's nothing to do with me,
my on-going desires. When I return
to the dining room, I find this single
anxiety, at least, unwarranted:
I am hovering after all, shadow
in a drafty door when the call comes,
and I attack your sweet greeting.

Apologia for Leaving

Leave the shirt unworn
on its wooden hook,
last cosmetics on a shelf.
Leave eggs unbroken
and the pot of tea, cold.
Leave persistent rain,
wind to its solace.
Leave the river explaining.
Let the door ring once,
once and be still.
For today she has flown,
she who won't return,
our beloved in her raven coat,
painful scarf of beauty.
Or rather it is he
who has parted—handsomely
adored, our true and only—
and furnished rooms
as sorrowful museums.
Or perhaps, early, unnoticed,
it's merely I who left.
Gone quietly forever.
As you will.

III: *The Brewer Introduction to Literature*

All I need for my ends
is your layer of dirt
and the long gone
smell of burning.

—*Wislawa Szymborska*

The Plums in the Icebox

Simply stated, you like to watch:
young woman stepping beyond the walls
of her husband's wooden protection,
shy outline of breast, of hips.
As you pass through leaves, red-faced
and red-handed, other men approach
with offers of fish, of ice.
It's no crime. You accelerate and bow.

On the square, a sad sack of a poor
old woman munches a plum that transforms
you both. She likes the taste—you could
say that again—of this ripe ruby
in her hand, the goodness she sucks out.

But those in the icebox, that you knew
perfectly well your wife saved
for breakfast, the ones she loves?
Sure you took them. She likes you more,
and your note, all charm and cheek,
is an apology you get away with.

Even now, you raise purple sphere
to lips, its sweaty cool, explode
sweet skin between teeth
in messy tribute to women young or old.
With your free hand, you navigate
with delicate precision for the hospital,
into oozing snapshots of spring,
this contagious country you adore.

But wasn't it fall just moments ago?
No matter. There aren't enough seasons,
enough mornings to focus through
rimless frames. Yes, everything depends.

And as for that wheelbarrow just passed,
still shiny with rain, those silly
white chickens? For God's sake.
Refrain for once from your labored
meanings. Let this last plum be enough.

Blue-Eyed Boy

You can't commit to any of this trinity—
Jesus, Wild Bill, Death—but lean for balance
inside the angles of that starry ring,
one boot grappling a stirrup of each trick pony
and gunplay to bring down the big tent.
So the papers said, and history doesn't lie.

But is that what you really came here to ask?
Whether Cody's cooked? It's the sure-sighted,
bull's-eye syntax of a titillatin' new world
that confuses you, the rubes on their feet.
Watch feathers fly. Quiz your earthly accountant.

As you polish sequined holsters between shows,
never mind a memory, faint but ever-finer,
of a pyramid of bones—buffalo, savage—
high as heaven, William reclined on cushion seats,
barrel on one thigh, glass of sweet bourbon
the other, everything a man needs in his lap.
That train's riding straight to the future.

Defunct, indeed. Same to you, hero, whatever
your name be now for the final show.

A Pretty Thing to Do

Was it all as you dreaded a sham, a fancy of youth?
That you were the one who would bark Swahili
like snapping necks, drink their Scotch
with a splash of disdain, face red and eyes frozen
blue in inhuman firelight? You the one
with the double cot to give the Yale boys'
wives their money's worth with a thrash inside the net?
To hold steady on the trigger and no time
for foolishness or weakness or that cruel, enameled
species Woman. It was pleasing, then, to think so.
So why do you wake now, a grown man
shivering inside a sweaty tent? Are you ashamed,
turning alone on the raft of your cot?

What in hell's wrong with you? You should've read
more carefully. Is that hyena laughing, lion lounging,
or a jungle's three verses of your own clammy fear?
But you don't know the Somali proverb,
do you?, rabbit, amateur with spent fortune.
The predator returns to lie with you, those good
breasts, tanned thighs, small-of-back-caressing hands
and you wonder, as you fall into a dream
of the men you've hated, if you're in the right story
in this unforgiving country. But there you stand,
accused, Springfield like lead in two wooden arms,
feet hammered to the earth, a rustle in the bush
and your head, your head ready to explode.

Only Insomnia

You stand before the unpolished bar
of the bodega with what spare dignity
one may muster for these hours.
What is the time? It is late, friend.
You stand, quietly alone in the residue

of a smile for a prayer of nothing.
You still see the old man, deaf
but nearly steady, departing the café,
vanquished to night and perhaps
a bed, perhaps a dreamless sleep.

You hope so. Other possibilities,
they are less good. And your confident
young friend, with humbling lessons
to learn—but not tonight, not tonight—
he is most certainly home, woman

soft against the angular certainties
of his body. Now you too, friend,
must leave, turn from the barman
who has turned from you, step cautiously
from these oblique and pleasant lights

and again toward the late shadows
of the trees. So late, in fact, it will
soon be early once more. How strange.
With dawn, perhaps you too shall
sleep, and that is all you ask of mercy.

Yes, the Amontillado

Always, you held with impunity the finish
of your foe, recognizing your own
in that fist. Fate's servant, trowel saluting
family shame, player raising a jagged bottle
of *de Grâve*—the sort of private joke
you relished in those days—to the lurid,
guzzling hole of clown masquerading

as connoisseur. You, who torched the way
through towers of bones, laughing inside.
Your motives perhaps obscure, method severe,
but he deserved it, you see, and so did you.
So when the troubling switch? When did
a dizzy head clear for one numb moment
of sight: you'd been the fool all along,

stumbling, impatient? Shackles stabbing puffy
ankles, wheeze sunk in the hollow
of your chest, eyes burning with dreams
of light. Not God, money, or jingle of bells,
muted in pitiful allegory, would rescue.
Where now your expertise, your insults?
Half a century gone, beyond the hole a whisper,

imagined in thin air, of your old accomplice.
You choke a final nitred cough—indeed,
you did not die of cough—listen calmly
to the tunnels' black refrain, a phantom's icy
whistle: *in pace requiescat.* Fortunately
he never did, never will. And if it's any
thematic consolation, neither did you.

The Food You Liked

Admit: you were one of the three butchers,
appointed nightwatcher to that shrill, shriveled
little man with his cage and clock.
Who else would you be? Fickle crowd?
Impresario, arms raised like a ringmaster,
wallet fat in his striped pants? Hardly.

See, you work for a living—knives, gristle, bone,
flesh on the block, blood on the smock.
There's your poetry and art. Maybe you think
that little man, aged child in gray
diapers on a pallet of straw, thin voice croaking
with old refrains you'd tried to forget,
maybe he'd stick in your thoughts.

He got smaller and smaller and named it genius.
You, meanwhile, were a rough man with hands,
thoughts to prove it. You hunched
on crates with your brothers in gore
and studied cards the torchlight dealt.
Some nights you couldn't believe he didn't snack,
most you didn't care. Who said life was fair?
More poetry. Those were long hours and still are.
You gnawed breakfast ham, sausages.
Joke on him, you stuffed the meat down.

Months later—or was it weeks, years?—after
you'd shoveled the "artist" into a hole,
young ones insisted you visit that panther.
You inspected the muscles under black velvet—
rib, loin, shank. The kids were shrieking
candy apples when it caught your eye. An image
entered in, plunged to its heart or maybe nowhere.

The Train that Brought You Here

In your production, it's not about fancy furs
and faux tiaras, polkas or magic lanterns,
the long parade to grave or a plantation, lost.
Study instead the spilled guts of that circus trunk:
poems of a dead boy, defiled in your hands;

a ream of legal hogwash from Ambler & Ambler,
who pecked at the bones. These yellow documents
indicate your bipolar dilemma: part Mitch,
part Stan. Part mama's boy, awkward in your skin,
sweaty in summer alpaca, silver lighter

fumbled in your hand and etched verse of loss
no talisman against the future. Then again,
you've got plenty of rooster in you, primary colors,
silk jackets, shirts, pjs, king and master,
deliverer of meat to the table. Plus, you clean up

nice and know it. So where do these boys
reconcile inside you?—Two-Forty-First Engineers,
grease monkeys grunting from the cave to see
how cards fall, who gets lucky. That's the drama.
A river of whiskey in the veins, redolence

of warehouse coffee and bananas, sticky-sweet,
attenuated decay put to music by a blue piano,
and, like in some old movie always played late,
two paws curled into fists, knuckles of one
tattooed "love," the other "hate." That's the moral.

And in the closing space between them: Blanche.

The Joys of Secret Sin

"For the Earth, too, had on her Black Veil"?
Can you blame her? The better to avoid
the humbug of these two soldiers of melancholy—
that young, good man who soils the world
with his dark dream; a sweat-lipped preacher
smugly trembling behind twin folds of crêpe.

The Earth doesn't appreciate her name
sullied—always, winds howling and bestial
cries. Women don't fare much better—
poor plump Faith, her pink ribbons disavowed;
long-suffering Elizabeth, left old by cryptic
evasions. Who in the village doesn't
recognize the human face or needs reminding?

Black veil on every visage? Dying hour of gloom?
That's the rectitude that compels them all—
deacon, farmer, child, maiden, hag—
toward your welcoming smile, avuncular wink,
kindly dip of black staff, so curiously
entwined it seems almost to writhe. There,
just ahead: the forest's mossy, crooked path,
a canopy of flames, a guiltless hearth of stone.

Preferring Not to

This lawyer who employed and implored you,
who scribed your history, this unnamed man
of proud prudence—he courts your forgiveness.
But for what? That's an answer he can't
decipher amid the careful loops and descenders
of documents, in accusing Wall Street walks.

Your "dead-wall reveries" haunted him,
so, of course, he betrayed you in self-defense.
Your silence of bared brick and mortar.
Your hungry art facing their beer-curses
and spleen. What if you were man, not symbol,
case study or ghost? Every wall is not a whale.

And your choice, offered to all counselors
in that office, all kings of a dead-letter
world? Not one of them listened. Sleep now.

Her Tippet, Only Tulle

The chariot spit-shined, horses' heads
steaming from there to eternity.
Your black suede and glowing
wingtips. You were styling when
you picked her up—thin girl, laced tight—
wallflower ready for petals to fall.

You took your time passing school kids—
sexy grain—paling arc of day—
all paths that led to your place.
"A Swelling of the Ground—" she whispered—
You said, show me your dark need.

You knew what the quiet ones wanted
and ripped a clawful of gossamer.
The eyes—the gasp—the blades of teeth—
You dug her. But you dig them all.
And like the rest—one date,
one rough harvest, she'd never leave.

Colosseum by Moonlight

Winterbourne—you assume the fateful irony
of the name, cold travel in foreign parts,
lonely, clock-work interiority of deliberation.
May thought and deed ever be conjoined?
Fluid consciousness and body stiff as an umbrella?
She could flash a cruel tongue, the unthinking girl.

Still and all, possibly you preferred her
to the dark matrons you feared in the dark city
where you thrived in Calvin's shadow? Who may say,
definitively? How may a gentleman, however long
from home, fathom fickle shades of an American flirt,
a simple type, more charming for an unfinished
prettiness, who always falls for the Italian.
The chance on offer—and what was *that* precisely?,
you allow, forgiving a smile—wasn't worth the risk.

Cite the horror at the Colosseum, should one require
further proof. You recall her in rare moments
between "studies," allow perhaps an impressionable
young man might have credited less an old aunt's
severities. But how, pray, might one ever
have distinguished the rapture of a girl's heart
from the hopeful and muted voice in one's head?

Dare to Eat a Peach

Who wouldn't feel for the man, bald head
on a platter causing even the women
who come and go, come and go, to chitter.
Wouldn't nod to a small, overwhelming need,
a question . . . derailed by dizzy
perfume, rustle of skirts, elegant wrist.

[Walt warned of the intoxicating
houses, the distillation of rooms.]
You're relieved when he leaves the party,
gossip, measurements of spoons . . .
too late, too late, for a purchase on sand.

They're smiling at skinny legs, or worse
not looking at all. Supporting player
dispatched in act three or forgotten
in drafty wings, old man straining after
[in the sea wind? briny toil of surf?]
an inhuman chorus, a chorus of beauty.
Who wouldn't recognize his meager despair?

But this lonely song is not your own,
for all its failure and footnotes.
This you tell yourself and, today, believe.
[Think instead of Pablo, scuttling
joyous claws across silent seas,
drinking the nutritious fishy truths.]

Alfred drowns either way. And you,
you'll study the proofs on screen
a longer while, while the universe remains,
shantih, quite singularly undisturbed.

A Hard Find

Soft body of Bailey Boy enraged by jagged spirit
of Misfit, that's your theory. That is, exterior life
of two brats and another learning how, wife with brains
of a cabbage and who knows what mother thinks,
batty old coot. Let a man just try to relax,
have some goofy fun, drive the clan down to Florida
like his own daddy did every spring like clockwork.

Just try to find peace or pleasure in this world.
Blue parrots on your shirt?—each a dutiful response
to job, home, every lousy day of your life.
Car flipped in ditch might as well tell the story.
As well off a monkey in a tree, fleas for gourmet.
No wonder your mind's a cloud. As you limp for the dark
woods, your last cry, though, is from mama's boy

to mama, that you'd return for her. Only that yellow
shirt came back, cassock draped across the Misfit's
bone-sharp shoulders, your other life, your spirit self—
philosopher, theologist, wounded animal escaped
from his cage and driving a coffin straight through
the heart of this dusty, bloody, misbegotten land.
You're tough, on the inside, searching for Jesus

in a blank sky, perfecting your cosmology of pain
endured and pain inflicted. Naw, that's just joking.
As said, you limp for that gaping mouth of blackness
—I'll be back, Mama! Mama, wait on me!—
son who's a stranger squeezing your sweat-slick hand,
mind blank as an empty pistol, and couldn't care less
what meanness means. Bailey Boy, inside and out.

Burning

A father accused, a son, a smell of cheese.
The boy on a keg of nails, feral gut twisted
with wanting. The Justice cracks the hammer,
case dismissed and they're back on the wagon,
the whole ragged family, busted stove,
silent clock pointing the way clear of town.

You study this wretched cycle, find yourself
when the father strikes you, his black immensity
carved in light of stingy fire, your second
beating of the day. He's wrong: *You'd have lied*
for him, you'd have done it. Twenty years
passed, you still taste that Snopes blood fierce

on your tongue, still hear the gunshots,
still walk a dream of black trees all around.
Twenty years and waking to the agonized truth,
your heart's pull and despair, waking cold
with the old man's limp. Whippoorwills still
predict the dawn as you walk the stiffness away.

Miss Emily's Men

You were not of course her father, crayon image
canted in a frown above Emily's procession to the grave.
Whatever you might prefer, you were no Homer Barron,
cigar clenched in his common Northerner's jowls,
reins and whip tight in the yellow glove
of another Sunday tempest, curtains of the town
quivering with gossip, pleasure, and appall.
Nor were you a very old man in Confederate splendor,
vague in time, recalling perhaps to have danced with her.
You were not Sartoris's ghost nor Negro servant.

No. Of the many satellites of men to their idol
—so alone, aloof, ironically complete in isolation—
you were merely one of the rest, slinking under darkness
at house's edge, sowing the cellar with your lime
and fear, animal, burglar, councilman, petty juror.
Breathing hard from the sanctuary of shadow
across lawn, you raised your head to her figure
as you would live it forever—limned and solitary
in its elevated frame, upright, motionless, vanquishing,
enigmatic and perverse. You crept to your room
to report what you'd witnessed and the smell went away.

And when at last the earth reclaimed her,
your anxious shoulder buckling the secret
of Emily's chamber, your nostrils were the first
to note an acrid, violated dust, your eyes to discern
in pallid rose light a single abiding hair on pillow.
The story long-finished, but now you'd be the one
—sibilant, covetous and failed—to try to tell it.

IV: Men, Building

The first completely free man will be the last one left on earth. He'll be able to do just whatever he likes, if he can think of anything.

—*Kingsley Amis*

Men, Building

Often, but not too, I steal a look
at my father and take account:
white t-shirt and suspenders, head down,
peppered hair broken loose from spray,
sawdust in the hair, permanently
dark and tattooed arms guiding saw
through veins of lumber.
I have studied this snapshot my entire
life, understand, sometimes standing behind,
steadying the horses, raising the cord
clear, blinking at dust.
Sometimes, but not often.

Once I taught my father the word
kerf, the emptiness the blade creates,
what's lost of the measure
while making the measure,
thinking it would interest him,
and it did. Halfway through the lesson,
however, I doubted my definition,
what the hell I was talking about,
and whether, really, such a word existed.

He looks up from the cut, tallying
numbers, feet and inches, calculating
in the sky the steps, missteps, implications.
Although I'm calling the shots
this time, picking up the tab,
he tells me just enough about what's next
that I won't be confused, or, possibly,
crucified by how far we have to go.

*   *

We are building this together,
father and adult son.
The Youngest and the Old Man,
Last Call, Hammer-and-Claw Cowboys,
writing our own savage laws of leverage,
weight, stability, force, finish.

Yippee. His idea, his insistence
for a parting gift. Eventually, I fall
for the perverse machismo of it,
eventually, brow-beaten and uncertain,
regretting the past, dreading the future,
I agree.

Someone should have reminded me
about the goddamned present. I decide
to be a man, be a mensch, suck it up,
but instead get drunk each night
as efficiently as possible,
avoid our usual talks, drop into bed early.
Stare at the ceiling of the next round.
The calendar meanwhile claims springtime,
if you care to believe what you read.

* *

Men arrive. Students, felonists,
Good Ole Boys who know concrete like
their own assholes. The job—
a grubby, unwashed, sharp-toothed beast—
is after all too big for us two.
We reluctantly welcome them and invite
more. And by god they arrive,
some with belts of tools and lunch coolers,
other with empty hands, blurry eyes.
We are stranded within a third-rate
Steinbeck. "Good fun and fair wages"

is the joke that gets around,
although I don't know who gets it,
who's listening, or whom it's on.
But everything's in cash,
and this, I believe, closes the case.

* *

When bare walls are upright
and leveled by eye, when rough-
covered trusses are steady, my father departs
with few words. No speech to the troops,
although they keep arriving:
electrician hired in a store aisle
by a man who'd heard about the job;
the stranger's brother, a huge, lonely,
clumsy Indian; another with his own skillsaw
(left-handed) and horses, who sells enchiladas
on the weekends, along with, one morning,
his young Mexican friend Bonito,
"con especialidad de stucco." *Bueno, àndale*,
I wave them in, spend days pacing the site,
hands on hips, thumbs tucked
into nail apron like, I imagine, a demanding
but benevolent ranchero, whatever—
who has time to quibble with dictionaries?—
just like someone possibly in charge,
El Hombre with Deep Pockets
vaguely disappointed by every effort.
"Worried" and "weary" I perform flawlessly.

My wife and I fill and refill
the money jar, and I empty it.
I quit keeping the lid on,
quit hiding it on a back shelf in the kitchen,
quit exchanging dollars for receipts.

Keep the machine rolling.

At night, pour.

*   *

Claudia does a wise and credible
job of steering clear.
Now and then, I see her obliquely,
walking the dog, leaving to shop
or lecture, and I am envious and amazed
at her strange, orderly life.
After I outlaw—for Christ's sake—
chilled bottles of spring water for the crew,
I hardly see her at all,
except for emergency bank runs.

*   *

My father returns once, and he and I
spend a long, slow weekend measuring,
accommodating, adjusting old pine 2"x8"s.
The wood is twisted, torturously hard to cut
and refuses both staple and nail.

I wasted a modest fortune
staining, painting, sealing samples.
Then we hung the salvaged wood as it was—
knotted, furry gray, marked with history
of insects and weather. It had lasted
nearly twenty-five years as is
and would outlast me without my help.

By the end of the weekend
I am shaking, too hung over
to think much about how my elderly father
feels climbing into his battered Buick

for the four-hour drive home.
Altogether, he has missed
more nights with my mother
than anytime during their 51-year marriage.
This time he takes his tools,
except for one extension cord
and a collapsed box of 16-penny nails.

The barn wood on the new gables,
by the way, is magnificent,
better than we dared imagine.

* *

So forth, so on. You only get one life,
you and me both, so I'll soon be merciful
and let you waste the rest of yours
as you will. Somewhere in the spiral,
think fortieth birthday.
Claudia on pins all day to avoid
The Wrath, lavishing me with smoked salmon,
truffle butter, caviar from
two types of domestic sturgeon,
good things of the earth
echoing vaguely back to some
comically pampered life, echoes awkward
in my hands and foreign in my mouth.
My old dog, whom I've hardly seen
during our favorite season, appears as magic,
and when I reach for his head
he allows me to touch the white fur
although I feel unpracticed, unworthy.

I get drunk again, good stuff
this time, but nevertheless. Then
I bawl like an idiot, Jesus, for absolutely

no reason I can name, throughout a favorite
dinner of duck and olives. Mostly
recover for the 1977 Madeira.
The next day's Monday, a working day.
The labyrinth, open for business.

* *

Why make a big deal out of nothing?
Think black-and-white prison film,
pages of calendar flying, flying
into fate's dizzy, deadening abyss.
One day, even Edward G. rolls his last load
of dingy sheets out of the stinking,
sweaty hell of the prison laundromat
and blinks up into a bright
orb in the sky, momentarily blinded.
A free man no longer a number, free and poor
until he puts together something better.
Let's get on with it.

* *

Sunday again, say the last
of April. Late afternoon and,
for effect, Edward G.'s sun again blazes.
Lilacs and tulips have passed
their primes, but irises are just snaking up
on thick scapes, roses just budding,
lilies hardly even begun. The day not perfect
but not total shit, either.

A man newly into middle-age stands
absurdly stained, torn, and repellent
in a uniform of proud humiliation

he quit washing weeks ago, awaiting
just this ceremonial day. His droopy jeans,
rotted at the crotch seam,
now expose his entire ass, one cheek
of his sad shorts browned—honestly—
with stain from a pocketed rag. It's too late
to care. For today, you see,
even as we watch, the man paints
with a roller the finish of his floor,
final official act of construction.

Of contrition? Ho ho, the man
remains clever, pleased to be alone,
but when his neighbor, retired archeologist,
strolls up unannounced, that's okay too.
He is Orpheus, he is Phoenix,
and he is feeling benevolent.
A witness is good. He tells the neighbor,
this tubby intellectual, to stand back,
get his muddy prints off the clean
foundation and, with a flourish,
our hero dips his wand, turns exposed
buttocks delicately from audience,
and pirouetting like a dancer
kisses the final raw inches
with the fur of the roller,
with the dark, glossy sealant.

The wardrobe, every piece including
socks and shoes, goes straight
into the trash, double-bagged for fumes.
Burning is too much trouble.
Who feels like a drink?

* *

So, I lied—there's more. This bitchy fellow,
showered, rested, whiskey exchanged
again for the beloved martini
emblematic of his easy life,
has one last trial to complete,
simple and ceremonial but important,
before mother and father arrive
to grade the final product. He sets
a slender glass with care on newly erected
and otherwise empty tool shelves,
drives a nail, straightens the artisanal
buffalo skull and steps back:
bravely substantial on daringly exposed
4"x4", raised from Tex-Mex textured walls
painted a subtle "sandtone," it hangs
cryptically at home. Between side door
and window he hammers again,
adjusts a small bamboo frame
fixing his father's initial drawing—
skeleton often and long-since extinct—
rendered simply and authorially
in rulered ink on common three-hole paper.
One gesture ironic, the other not.

So he stands centered on a bare floor—
son; husband; pussy; big disappointment;
in short, da Vinci's ideally flawed mechanism,
study of the finite, sketch of diminished capacity,
years hardening already his, the baby's,
bones, between a trail of irretrievable past
and terrible, blurry arc of future—
stands, that is, swallowing hard
on an olive, stuffed personally. He wonders
what his dad will think. What they
still might have to say, and for how long.

V: Home Fires

Come down off the cross
We can use the wood.

—Tom Waits

Few love to hear the sins they love to act.

—William Shakespeare

Blackberries

What if the road were a metaphor
for a road, a single curving lane of nowhere,
and the sky for a leaden sky.
What if, moreover, brambles represented

brambles, barbwire a rusted steel,
and each berry unattainable on the other side
a dark conception of itself.
What then of the young buck and his mate,

startled and, in leaping turns,
departing the field unseen. What of the great
bird calling from a barren climb
and the molting rattler, its blind strike

the mythology informing each step.
What of the figure of a man roving cautiously,
the price of hand and arm submitted
to thorn, how for days to follow

flesh will return these intrusions.
What of theoretical salt burning eyes,
symbolic shirt stained to chest, and later,
at last, what of that first taste,

ripeness judged sweet but not, perhaps,
to her thematic tongue, quite sweet enough.

Dinner Out

No crème brûlé these days, be serious.
So once your places are cleared
it's just the matter of payment—
too damn much—splitting what's due,
negotiating a margin of service:
stick it to the girl or pile it on,
or division that cuts where it should.

Some small change finally arrives
and the rest's a figurative cakewalk:
the wave to the owners—good-bye,
good-bye, thanks ever so much—
out with a flourish or stumble.
Couples preened for the night two-step
toward bars, intersect your course.

"Too old for that," she concludes,
thus knotting a bow around evening's
conversation, a Gordian noose,
a what-the-hell-ever: just shut up.
The top down exposes skulls to heaven,
rebuke of wind you vowed was fun.
Then it's eyes on the road, knuckles on

the wheel, the yellow line home
with no flashing lights or ironic gods,
only a shameful, searing déjà vu
and a hundred silent conceits
bubbling the swamp of your brain
that it will never, ever happen again,
whatever it is, or was, or shall be.

Duck Confit

4:06 a.m., late July, two blue feet bare
on carpet in a refrigerated bedroom,
is no time to ponder class prerogatives.
Nor is 4:08, kitchen bulbs lengthening doorways,
appropriate to reflect upon effete habits,
or decades of your mother risen in the dark
to tent a bloated November bird in foil
and heat while the house slept, by god, soundly.
4:11 I can assure you is no time for indulgence,
for silliness, to rethink life's bargain.
It is the moment, instead, glasses askew,
to lift each thigh from overnight caress
of garlic, fresh bay leaf, home-harvested thyme,
to massage flesh under cold water
with priestly certainty, free all excess of salt,
lay each upon its pallet of skin and fat.
4:15, moreover, is time for concubine
to administer olive oil bath, up to the top
and one quarter inch more for decadent measure,
four cups of green virgin, first-press,
sampled from drowsy fingertips to drowsy lips.
Priest, concubine, virgin? 4:17 subdued to 200°,
think merely some thought of this sort:
14 hours remain between toil and ascendance.
Creaking hinge of a dual-oven stove,
door raised to closure. An expectant silence.
4:19, however, dog's distant wheeze
unheard from your master bed, blazing day to come
still only suspicion behind any woods
looked to for solace, 4:19, when one may lower
a switch and night commence its imponderable
strategy—that's another story altogether.
Think then what you will, once work is done.
And sleep again, sweet prince, if you're able.

Tips for the Martini Diet

Don't concern yourself with chewing
slowly or what you believed you ever knew.
Do swallow what's in your mouth
before the next sip.

The third week, or third year,
often marks a diet plateau. This is due
to rebalance of water loss. Eliminate
the olive, its unnecessary brine,
to give yourself that push off the edge.

Make each drink an occasion. In dieting
appearances do count. A newly frosted glass,
fresh ice, jaunty shake and pour.

Pinpoint periods (other than happy hour)
when you're most likely to go off your diet.
Plan something (jogging, tennis)
that keeps you from martinis at that time.

Note above: kidding. Guard your sense of humor.

Commit to the diet. Once you've selected gin,
give it a chance, even a lifetime.
Don't abandon it for another type of diet
(rum, vodka, bourbon) you think might prove better.

Do your shopping after you've been
drinking, never before. Traveling
liquor store aisles when you're parched
can lead to overbuying all the wrong kinds
of impulse booze. (Sake anyone?)

Fill spare time. Sign up for a course
at your local school, do volunteer work,
get involved in a community, political, or . . .

alright, enough joking. Just remember
that evenings will need to be free
of other commitments. In the mornings,
too, you'll often be unavailable.

During the pressure of a social or family
dinner, don't resist. Politely ask
that your plate and utensils be removed;
better still, just announce you won't be coming.
It will tempt less to stay away.

Take a thermos to work. You'll discover it easier
to meet your diet quota for lunch.

When you crave a martini at the wrong time,
some say chewing a thin slice of lemon or lime
helps. You may find that a gin & tonic
with a double twist brings the right relief.

Encourage your spouse to drink with you,
so you can plan together and offer
mutual encouragement.

Redecorate! Refinish the bar, buy new
thin-stemmed glasses, stainless tongs and bucket.
Since your body is getting a new look,
this is a great time to perk up surroundings.

Drink no water, ever (except buckets at night).
Trust your martini to satisfy appetite, facilitate
excretion, cleanse your temple of impurities.

Think of a better shape as well as thinner one.
When exercising your wrist, concentrate
on trouble spots: abdomen, waist, hips.
The past, the present, the future.

Don't sacrifice nutrition. Being slim is pointless
if you're ill. Your diet should avoid empty
calories and include nutritional balance
from all food groups. Skip dips and cheeses.
Spear the maligned olive back in.

Blunt hunger with a pre-menu "cocktail."
A half hour before your first,
down a chilled shot.

Each time you crave a drink and don't have it,
estimate the cost, put the money in a secret place.
At the end, upgrade to a case of premium brand
you can't usually afford.

When mixing, remember that herbs and botanicals—
for instance juniper, coriander, angelica—
add zest to a bland existence.

Try this instead of a bedtime "snack": snarl
at spouse and pet, then step into the dark
and glare at the moon. Stumble in aimless circles
beneath a black skeleton of trees.

Forget the word "failure."
If you slip up occasionally—
redouble your efforts, don't use it as excuse
to stop drinking altogether. Nobody's perfect.

Entertaining at home, serve rich sauces
and dressings on the side, or burn it all
and throw the shit away. Then, you can diet
without interruption (your guests will be
appreciative, too).

As your confidence grows and results begin
to show, diet for the whole day,
not just a few hours in the evening.

Make a list of your "martini friends," people
you usually meet for drinks. One after another,
as they begin bicycling or pilates class,
join the church or have children,
cross them off the list.

If you should get depressed or discouraged
or feel betrayed or worthless,
imagine all the activities
your new appearance will allow.

Try this: visualize yourself a supple blade
in that wardrobe of torn shorts and stained
shirt, staggering barefooted off the porch.
You're so thin your loved ones hardly
recognize you. Weaving in the twilight,
just look at you, barely there at all.

Ashes

The first surprise is how angrily
logs answer, as if every punishing season
locked together prophesied consummation.
We couldn't save the Rembrandt or the cat,
resolve forensic stupidities
or ever after learn the cause. Instead,
I limped the endless gravel drive, feet bare,
wheezing like a shot wolf, then stopped.
Where was I going? This was our isolation
mortgaged and worshipped. I breathed the moon.
I felt flame on my back and turned.

That's the next surprise, unfathomable heat.
I squatted beside my wife weeping
in the grass. I worried of our vulnerability
to chiggers—it had been a murderous year—
hoped blaze sufficient to save our skin.
Then I thought again randomly of books,
photographs, letters, so much paper
returning to essence. My poems, every last one.
I couldn't. I couldn't get through the door,
and I thought it spoke little of me
a thin manuscript came foremost to mind.

Red tongues, hydrangeas rows of sticks.
Blistered pole of the cherry we planted.
My face burning. As I touched my wife, her sobs
soared to the inchoate woods, the eyes
watching us watch. No human neighbors showed.
I crouched, dripping, shaking, tried to raise
Claudia from the infested ground
and speak usefully, somehow, above the roar.
That's the third surprise, conquering voices
of the fire, and it felt forever before
I heard the first faint, responding siren.

Dark Night

I won't insist on purplish bruises
of sky defining soft hills,
nor that evening air cooled
feverish temperatures we had dined on.

Where would such contrivances lead?
That the faint plates of mist
hovered in foggy apprehension,
each rare headlight beam
blazed its threat of entrapment?

Let's keep motions simple,
eyes straight, wheels lawful between
the lines. Foolish, but wary.
In 17.4 miles the road ended where it ends.

The hills black now. The miles
cold comfort of isolation.
I faced a choice of north, south,
or back the way I'd come.
Thus the decision on nights like these—
obvious, neither here nor there.

Later, route dimly lit and my head
blurred, I nearly passed the blind curve
—make nothing of that—marking
the dead-end street—leave it, won't you?—
of our home. Then, almost too late
to turn, I saw the sign revealed.

First Day out of the Box

This morning the artist earmarked
for a landscape of that imagined evening
when every loss he'd engineered
focused into a single determining point.
Something like that. It occurred to me

last night, wheeling home with the top down,
thick summer air slapping me silly.
A bleak idea just my kind of thing.
Now, though, as I prepare to apply first
black strokes to canvas, I am distracted
by the hungry, alternating chirps

of baby bluebirds, fuzzy heads just visible.
Visible enough, however, and as I adjust
field glasses, goofy avuncular smile
etched in place, I am pleased but concerned
by the buoyant lack of discretion,

proximity of a pair of floppy, grounded
bodies to the fenced boundary of woods.
So as the anxious mother beaks a grasshopper
down the throat of who's next, then hesitates,
blinking, exposed, pale and beautiful,
and I join the father's watch,

that terrible tableau of pride and cost,
defeated on my knees beneath blind moon
or fist raised under inky deafness,
will have to wait. It arrives soon enough
in dark-feathered finery, no doubt.

But for now the hatchlings won't shut up
about their fear, joy, need. Luckily for them
the god of this valley is a big admirer,
although his felicities are said to be
self-occupied, and his mercies,
granted, to be famously fleeting.

Blueberries and Corpses

Putrescence first, or affronting heat,
or something not right along the wild wall
I hack and curse to hold my place.
Honeysuckle has forced the fence to its knees.

Unpronounceable oven of air. By then
the rot inside me, in nostrils and lungs,
thick-spiced aromatic of death
that can't be confused. And flies, angry,

dizzying at ankles, gyring heavenward
to neck, ears, eyes. I follow the scent home,
it is close behind, close beneath
this untamed deck adjacent to bushes:

furred remains of lobes, softness
humming and trembling with activity,
generous, congealed host. Sticks splinter
in the flat weight before I surrender

to what I know: one slick, opalescent ear
pressed between thumb and finger,
most of the churning mess raised clear
of steps. I'm fortunate skin holds.

Ten paces and I toss it all
underhanded beyond the fallen fence.
Anything inside those woods that cares to look
can see me plainly, exposed man

with left hand curled before his face,
man breathing. To scrub the scent now
is pre-emptive, pointless. At the bushes
I ignore the disrupted flies and with my right

pluck each ashy-dark berry that remains.
It's late season but I harvest
an awkward fistful. Then I kick the door in
and enter with spoils to announce.

The Hunter and the Figs

> . . . the things of the night cannot be explained
> in the day, because they do not then exist . . .
> —*Ernest Hemingway*

Victimizing a final slice of fig tart
and morning's first hot cup—the best one—
I have failed so far to banish the night,
light flashing curtain, on the floor
holding my old dog as he trembled.

For a decade he was fearless of thunder,
then he wasn't. We lay a long while,
panting, whispering, waiting for calm.
Outside that ecstatic window we sniffed
long-eared remains, and I have been preoccupied

with the killer's identity, roaming cat
or young hawk lately whistling over roof.
This matters nothing to rabbit, or dog,
or storm. I say again it is morning,
the mutt has emptied himself and come in happy.

Hot earth has cracked. The rain
never arrived, only fury without relief.
For the tart, my wife supplied crust
and buttery cream, I figs from the season's
first raid on the Baptists. I parked

in a spot reserved for "Minister of Music,"
filled cooler with dark, warm handfuls of loot.
Somewhere I have lost my trepidation.
There's no more time for foolishness.
The last bite, and a dish to be licked clean.

Repair

Gummy wood yields so easily to thumb.
How had he overlooked that permeating stain.
The knife prods the log, penetrates,

blade raising water from sodden grain.
He begins to cut, pull at wet striations,
drop them where they fall. He saws thick skin

of chinking, tears loose surgical strips,
fistfuls of insulation. Then soft into dry rot,
more ruin spread from a single dark spot.

How could he have been so dull, inattentive.
He crouches as pine crumbles in his fingers,
tunnels of infestation collapse to dust.

A life in blinders. He is on his knees
relishing destruction, perverse exactitude,
this work of revelation gouging what firmness

remains, excavating cancer and beyond.
August, month from hell. Shards fly, he carves
to bone, feels a cold interior draft.

There, the hole where a wall stood complete.
There the exposed room, jaggedly framed
an absence he had imagined to be his solid home.

Through to the other side. Nothing to repair.

One for Willy Loman

Not until next afternoon,
uneasy in my cushioned chair,
did I make the troubling connection—
me in the yard at 4:00 am,
animated under the moon's guidance,
collecting fallen branches.

I mumbled my litany of self-defense,
resolution, settled scores.
Why not? The night was cool,
sky not yet squeezed shut
by progress. No one called my name.
I didn't see Willy there then,

gibbering right beside me
on his patch of dirt, parceling
carrot seeds, radishes,
lettuce in silly, ordered rows,
negotiating some profitable demise
with the ghost of a brother.

How could I have missed him?
As a student, I believed the old man's
delusions pathetic, even,
it embarrasses me, earned.
Some nights now we come close
to closing the sale. Which occurred

to me in the afternoon, as I say,
when I laughed, a good forgiving dose,
and went out to water the garden.

Hemingway This Morning

"I will tell you. It is not so simple."

He tumbles to his feet, into the day,
grizzled bear thirsty for answers.
His fourth wife, or first, whichever,
has wiped clean the basin counter,
an act he distrusts. The man leans
eye level to the canisters on his side,

lined in a gauntlet at cliff's edge,
and can't help recalling the Fascists:
there, cylindrical cap of mouthwash
resembling the hat of popinjay
Don Faustino, pitchforked beyond priest,
or squat aftershave not unlike

potbellied Don Anastasio, bludgeoned
beneath the cathedral of his hands.
"Left" and "right" of contact lenses,
toothpaste and razor prostrate already.
Such a short, final stumble
over the precipice, into the bin,

or with a flick of cruel hand
sent hurtling past powder puff and tissue
into abyss of cold commode
from whence none and nothing return.
Whiskey to scald ants on a burning log.
Later, outside, he works the blower

with the precision of the muleta,
hip thrust with a taunt, he fancies,
echoing Ordoñez. As the fallen swirl
in a horn of wind he dances back,
capturing all again in his stoic gale,
the ballet of dangerous autumn.

Wolves, Bears, No Cops

More than once, during coldest hours
of these astrological nights,
we've heard the trucks across the mountain.
But they've not arrived yet,
the monsters of our reckoning,
and my boys and I live still the brilliant
moments we were born to. Wood fire, smoke,
slow flame of bourbon, flesh

of game bird licked from salty fingers.
Laughter and story. Woods veiled
as in fable, contour of hills
beautifully fatal. Some tattered wildness.
We are all hunter and prey.
Tooth, claw, commune of yellow eye,
truth laid bare. Heaven's law, ashes.
And the steel jaws coming won't be sated.

A Wealth of Options

This morning I am conflicted between,
as I promised myself, a pyrotechnic
of ignited verses or, now that I've replaced
the thermostat fuse and installed
the long-anticipated and finally arrived
turbo-jet motor, 1.5 muscular horses,

going out into the cold to get my feet wet
in a final rubdown of the hot tub.
Mechanical frustrations have delayed
the christening of this year's naked season,
and already we have wasted full moon
and anniversary, with few options but

to languish dry and fully clothed,
stare at the sky, accept a peck on cheek
or bottle of Scotch. Too, I could
scrap plans and simply continue to admire
my numinous old dog, whom I never tire
of looking at or, as you know, writing about,

who just moments ago nosed his way
into the room and patiently allowed
a rub of magic belly, almost ridding
me of last night's wretched dream
involving his age and the house I grew up in.
Between peeks at his finery as he snoozes

on a pillow, I might open again the dizzying
rhymes I bent my head to this morning
for ballast, if not necessarily balance,
as for the second time in a month
I had to stop reading to search out
the word chthonic, *thän-ik*, from the Greek,

meaning infernal, as in "chthonic deities."
As I confirm this with Jasper he raises
an eyebrow, partially opens dark conjurer's
doggy eyes, and lets his tongue loll,
which I interpret to mean that this concludes
the poetry portion of our show and also

as prompt that so much water will take hours
to heat, which new fuse and motor
I pray will facilitate, to proper feverish
pitch for the raucously roiling chthonic
human stew I prefer, and time, Jasper reminds
me always, is for living and for play.

The Woman

> I would be very honored if you would compose a poem as part of the manuscript of my book, about the search of a man for his apparently disappeared girlfriend. The girlfriend, so it seems, only exists in his distorted mind. So it seems . . .

We never believed a word, at the beginning.
The night she rose, smoothed silk across her thighs,
and walked silently—*purposely*, he had stressed—
into the narrow woods, apparently out of this world
forever. Other times an airport was involved,

a seashore, a hushed language, one he had spoken
in childhood but forgotten; once, an abduction.
No price was ever demanded, no condition met.
We'd never seen her, any of us, except through
the film flickering behind his eyes. *Mise-en-scene*

of bottle and two glasses, ashtray, spent cigarette
stained stone-hearted red, drowsy fan overhead
confessing nothing but dust. And though we wearied
of him, banished his banalities and his phantoms,
we couldn't stop the telephone from tolling:

4:03 a.m.: he was certain he'd seen her at a club,
dipping into a limousine; 5:21: the trail lost
in shadow; 7:18: maybe it wasn't her, he can't
think anymore, but Christ that dress!, that hair!,
the curve of shoulder! It could have been her twin!

Then one morning the call we'd expected, flat voice
describing altercation, violence, his arrest.
It was over. Even then we didn't believe a word
and when he asked for us pretended not to hear.
We had our own ghosts to interrogate, our own story.

His pitiful, private journey a delusion complete.
Until the night the doorbell rang, with an urgency,
a strangeness, a threat we couldn't name, then.
Too late for a visitor. What was ever as it seemed?
And that for us was the end of the beginning.

www.ingramcontent.com/pod-product-compliance
Lightning Source LLC
LaVergne TN
LVHW050936080826
845145LV00004B/1290

* 9 7 8 0 9 7 7 7 1 8 2 3 8 *